daphne GUINNESS

daphne GUINNESS

BY VALERIE STEELE AND DAPHNE GUINNESS

FASHION INSTITUTE OF TECHNOLOGY NEW YORK | YALE UNIVERSITY PRESS NEW HAVEN AND LONDON

Designed by Paul Sloman

Printed in Italy

LIBRARY OF CONGRESS CATALOGING-IN-PUBLICATION DATA

Steele, Valerie.
Daphne Guinness / Valerie Steele and Daphne Guinness.
p. cm.
Includes bibliographical references and index.
ISBN 978-0-300-17663-6 (cloth : alk. paper)
1. Guinness, Daphne, 1967- 2. Fashion—History—20th century. 3.
Fashion—History—21st century. I. Guinness, Daphne, 1967- II. Title.
TT505.G85S74 2011
746.9'2—dc23
2011021879

A catalogue record for this book is available from The British Library

FRONTISPIECE

Daphne Guinness, wearing silver cat suit by Alexander McQueen.
Video hologram featured in the exhibition *Daphne Guinness*.
Photograph: The Museum at FIT.

CONTENTS

From her signature platinum-and-black striped hair and notorious eight-inch platform shoes to her to-die-for couture collection and amazing diamond jewelry, Daphne Guinness is the very image of rarified personal style. Upon first seeing her, many people must have asked themselves a variant of Guy Trebay's rhetorical question, "Who is this woman, what form of rara avis bedecked in diamonds and plumes?" She is often described as a fashion or style icon, sometimes as a muse, a couture princess, or the fashion person's fashion person.

"Daphne is one of – if not the – most stylish women living," says designer Tom Ford, who asked her to model in his Spring 2011 fashion show. "Life is a stage for Daphne," says the couturier Valentino. "Funerals or balls, she always makes a performance." The world has many beautiful, fashionable socialites and celebri-

FRANÇOIS NARS

NARS Fall/Winter 2010–11 Ad Campaign.
Daphne's dress by Nina Ricci
and headpiece by Philip Treacy.
Photo courtesy François Nars/
The Collective Shift/
trunkarchive.com

ties, but Daphne is in a class of her own. As her friend the art historian John Richardson puts it, "She is the object of her own creativity. Her persona is her own masterpiece."

Why do a book and exhibition on Daphne Guinness? Because she is fearless about wearing the most extreme clothes and shoes, but is no mere clothes horse; because she is a serious collector of couture, yet is also a creative force in her own right; because she is an extraordinary individual whose perspective on fashion is unique and important.

We tend to think of fashion as being created by fashion designers. Yet designers do not create in isolation. Every act of creation is a collaboration that takes place within a particular milieu, be it the art world or the fashion system. Amanda Harlech, Karl Lagerfeld's aide-de-camp and muse, has said that "Karl is continually inspired by [Daphne]." Valentino has described her as "the most creative person I know who is not a designer," praising her ability to "make something exciting out of something classic." Although designers bear primary responsibility for creating and proposing new looks, the story does not end there. In order for something to become fashionable, to move off the runway and into real life, it has to be taken up by various fashion insiders, including editors, photographers, retailers, and fashion trendsetters. The fashion or style icon is a special type of fashion insider, someone who is far more than an "early adopter" or celebrity clothes horse. The fashion icon not only inspires fashion designers and validates their clothes, but actually creates a look that affects the way other people dress and/or think about dressing. Michelle Obama, Kate Moss, Sarah

NICK HAYMES

Daphne wearing vintage Chinese jacket
and platform shoes by Massaro.
Photo Nick Haymes.

Jessica Parker, Lady Gaga, Rachel Zoe, Alexa Chung, Carine Roitfeld, and Daphne Guinness are all often described as fashion or style icons, as are historical figures such as Jacqueline Kennedy, Audrey Hepburn, Grace Kelly, Edie Sedgwick, and Gabrielle "Coco" Chanel. Actresses and singers, First Ladies and fashion models, editors, stylists, socialites, and the occasional designer are apparently most likely to be characterized as fashion icons. But what does this problematic term really mean?

An icon was originally an image of a sacred person worshipped by his or her followers. There is undeniably an element of enthusiasm bordering on worship in the popular response to celebrities. Consider the blog imtheitgirl.com referring to "style-icon-daphne-guinness": "There are normal people and there is Daphne Guinness. Ms. Guinness is the ultimate fashion fantasy where everyone wears couture 24/7 and has ridiculously perfect bone structure. I like this world and therefore I love Daphne." She also proudly quoted *Vanity Fair* journalist A. A. Gill, who argued that "[Daphne Guinness] has never had a look, never once, never remotely, that was anyone's but her very own."

This individualism, often described as eccentricity, is at the heart of Daphne's appeal. Equally important is her respect for the art of fashion. She has famously said: "We need better things, not more. We should not pollute the world with meaningless, unused things when we can make and support things of rare and precious beauty." And she puts her money where her mouth is, being one of the few celebrities who actually buys her clothes instead of borrowing them. As she told a journalist for *The Sunday Times*, "I

MARIO TESTINO

Daphne wearing Christian Lacroix
haute couture; epaulettes by
Alexander McQueen. Photo
by Mario Testino/Art Partner
for *Vogue* UK, March 2008.

don't understand why celebrities can't buy their own clothes. Elizabeth Taylor would never have dreamt of letting anyone tell her what to wear, yet nowadays they're all styled by someone else."

There have been many books and exhibitions on individual fashion designers, but surprisingly few on the women who have made their clothes come alive, and still fewer on women like Daphne who have patronized many designers in the course of creating a personal style of their own. Among the exceptions have been exhibitions (and books) on Tina Chow, Jackie Kennedy, Grace Kelly, Mona Bismarck, Iris Apfel, and Nan Kempner. Daphne Guinness certainly belongs in this company. Indeed, I think that any good history of fashion must take into account the importance of those individuals known as style icons.

Over the past year, Daphne and I have had many conversations exploring her life in fashion, and I have read everything that I could find about her, including commentary on the internet, where she has a devoted following. In addition, I have talked to a number of her friends, colleagues, and family members. I have also had the pleasure of going through Daphne's closets in New York and London. But this book is not about her personal life, except in so far as it relates to her personal style. If I asked about her childhood, for example, it was because I felt sure that the origins of her style went back to her earliest years.

*

JOE LALLY

Daphne wearing dress of her
own design. Photo Joe Lally.

The Honorable Daphne Suzanne Diana Joan Guinness was born in 1967, the daughter of brewery heir Jonathan Guinness, Lord Moyne, and French beauty Suzanne Lisney. Her paternal grandmother was Diana Mitford, one of the legendary Mitford sisters. Daphne is the youngest child in her family; she has an older brother, Sebastian, and three half-siblings (her father's children with another woman). She grew up in stately homes in England and Ireland, and spent summers with her mother in an eighteenth-century former monastery in Cadaqués, Spain, where Salvador Dalí was a neighbor.

In 1987, at the age of nineteen, Daphne married Spyros Niarchos, who was twelve years her senior and the second son of the fabulously wealthy Greek shipping tycoon Stavros Niarchos. A year later, she had the first of their three children. According to all accounts, they lived in a gilded yet constrained world, surrounded by bodyguards, traveling by yacht or private jet between homes in St. Moritz, New York, and the family's island in Greece. After her divorce in 1999, Daphne resumed her maiden name, and over the past decade she has emerged on the world's stage as this extraordinary fashion creature.

Daphne with her brother, Jasper.
Photo courtesy Daphne Guinness

JOHN RICHARDSON ON THE GUINNESS FAMILY

Bryan Guinness married the beautiful Diana Mitford, who left him for Sir Oswald Mosley, leader of the British Union of Fascists. While her grandmother was alive, Daphne "never read any books about her," she told Lucy Cavendish. "Every time I do now I feel horrified because what I read seems different to the person I knew . . . She was unbelievably nice, warm, friendly and most extraordinary. She was the biggest influence in my life, so I find it very complicated and very sad. I have spent my life trying to piece together that puzzle. I wish I could figure it out."

"That Daphne is a Guinness is important, because the Guinnesses are more than just a family. They are a vast international club. Whether they are enormously rich or penniless, old or young, famous or infamous, gay or straight, they have that special charisma quite unlike any other family. It has to do with their fundamental Irishness and all that involves: leprechauns, the gift of gab, not to mention the magic brew that the family still provides. As well as espousing aristocrats and plutocrats, they have been known to marry way beneath them."

DAPHNE ON HER MOTHER AND GRANDMOTHER

In addition to her paternal grandmother, Daphne's mother was an especially important fashion influence. But as she explains, there were quite a number of women in her life who were extraordinarily creative when it came to fashion.

I am blessed by an interesting heritage. My mother [Suzanne Lisney] grew up in France and Spain, and I was aware from a very young age that she was markedly different from other 'English' mothers. She was simply elegant, which is not a trait that is usual for the English. She wore suits and very well cut dresses in that clean and simple 1960s way.

My father's mother, my grandmother, Diana Mitford, was also like that, very crisp-looking. She always looked incredibly chic – tall and thin, in clothes which had a uniformity to them. Maybe that has quite a lot to do with my tendency to simplify, because even though things might look very complicated, in fact everything is always based on something simple.

From left to right: Daphne's mother, Suzanne Lisney; father, Jonathan Guinness; grandmother, Diana Mosley; and grandfather, Bryan Guinness. Photo courtesy Daphne Guinness.

My father doesn't really think about his dress. He really doesn't care. If he can't find a belt, he will tie his trousers with a piece of string. His whole world is books and the realm of the mind.

In the country in England, my mother used to store her clothes in the attic, and I'd go through everything and play dress-up. Once I found this cupboard; it was like Narnia! There were amazing things that belonged to my mother! I remember tiny shoes, very pointed and narrow with pom poms on them.

The Duchess of Windsor and Mona Bismarck were friends of my grandmother. Her sister Nancy [Mitford] loved clothes. My aunt Mariga [H.S.H. Marie-Gabrielle of Urach] was quite extraordinary looking. She was my father's brother's first wife – a very great talent, extraordinarily creative. She could quite literally turn one dress into another as if by magic by adding a feather or any such thing that may have been at hand. There were quite a number of women in my life who were like that, so to me that was quite normal. What they did was about creativity, not trying to show off how much money they had. That has always seemed vulgar.

BRYAN ADAMS

Daphne's coat by Louis Vuitton, dress by Alexander Mcqueen, earrings, Daphne's own, scarf, vintage. Originally featured in *Zoo Magazine*, issue 29, November 2010. Photo Bryan Adams/ trunkarchive.com.

ON BEING A GYPSY

As a child, Daphne lived in many very different places, including an artists' colony in
Spain, and this peripatetic existence had a
profound influence on her worldview. As she
told Frances Wasem, "It's funny how the
way you get wired as a child can really influence your whole life. I suppose I'm still
living the life of a gypsy."

I was visually curious at a very young age, not exclusively about fashion but art, landscapes, armor, architecture, light and transformations, because we were living in many different places. In Paris, we visited my grandmother and she was simple and elegant. Her world was books. Whereas in Spain there were, for a start, the hippies and all these quite strange people that had come like pilgrims to be near Salvador Dalí. They weren't strange to me, but I could tell they were different from the locals. You had artists and writers there, but also fishermen, and traditional families who wore Spanish dress, which was deeply fascinating. My mother was at her best in Cadaqués – these were her people. Then I would go back to England, where men and women wore hats right up until the late 1970s.

ON SALVADOR DALÍ

Dalí was a friend of my mother. I remember that he kept lobsters in his pool and he also had an ocelot, which was quite amazing. Someone in his entourage once threw the ocelot at my mother! Dalí had a fisherman's boat painted black that he paddled around in. You think his paintings are surreal, and, of course, they are, but the topography and the light around Cadaqués is extraordinary. Whenever Dalí came out, there would be a procession following him – a whole circus. Anything went, clothes-wise.

BRYAN ADAMS

Daphne's dress by Gucci and cape by
Giorgio Armani. Originally featured in
Zoo Magazine, issue 29, November
2010. Photo Bryan Adams/
trunkarchive.com.

ON NANNIES

In England, the nannies in the park were dressed in uniforms. But times had begun to change. The old-fashioned nannies wore little hats, rather like Mary Poppins, but the young nannies, in their twenties, wore the new fashions. That was their uniform. When I was really little, I had a Japanese nanny. My mother says I could speak Japanese then, but maybe she exaggerated. However, my fascination with everything Japanese started there.

ON BIBA

My mother knew Barbara [Hulanicki] and when I was about five we lived right next door to [her boutique] Biba. My nanny used to take me to Biba to see the flamingos on the roof. It was great! Biba was always packed with teenagers, and there were all these cool people milling around, and incense was everywhere. I would come home from school and beg to go there.

ON PLAYING DRESS UP

When I was a child, playing dress-up was so much fun. You could be a knight one day and an Indian the next.

MIKAEL JANSSON

Daphne wearing Givenchy by Riccardo Tisci jacket, top, and shoes with her own pants (purchased at a Dublin punk shop) and jewelry, 2009. Photo © Mikael Jansson.

ON UNIFORMS

I was quite a tomboy, always covered in mud or falling out of a tree. I had quite a lot of hand-me-downs from my brothers. I hated dresses, loathed them. I liked my sailor suit. But I really longed to wear a uniform. We didn't have uniforms at the first school I attended. I got my first uniform when I was eleven years old, and as I grew, it just got shorter and shorter. When I got it, the hemline was down to my ankle, and when I left, it was up to my thigh.

I *adored* uniforms! I was so jealous of my brother, because he went to Eton – and got to wear tails every day! I wished I had been born a boy – it seemed so unfair.

ON SLOANE RANGERS AND PUNK ROCKERS

There was a phenomenon known as Sloane Rangers, a kind of princess-bride look; the first example that springs to mind is Lady Diana. It was loathsome to me. I wanted to have my hair dyed black, red, and blue. When I was in boarding school, whenever I wasn't in uniform, I was getting stuff from Kensington Market, which was full of punk rockers. I was in leather from head to foot whenever possible.

ON HER CONFIRMATION DRESS

I remember going to get my confirmation dress, and I ended up buying a black taffeta dress. When I got to school, the headmistress said "You are not wearing that dress," and I said, "What do you mean? What's wrong with it?" So I was dispatched to buy this horrible Laura Ashley dress. But I had the presence of mind to rearrange it to make it look like a nineteenth-century wedding dress with a bustle, sort of Henry James or Tissot style.

ON BUYING AND MAKING CLOTHES

When I was fifteen or sixteen, I was absolutely passionate avbout Azzedine [Alaïa], wheedling ten quid here or there so I could buy some of his tight little black dresses. I was always in debt to everyone, because I didn't have much of an allowance. Once I went to a race, and I thought I looked perfectly acceptable, but I was in a studded leather skirt with a studded leather jacket and some sort of lace tights and stilettos. No floral hat. It did not go down well. I was told to tone it down.

What I didn't buy, I made. I made a dress once out of bin bags – I thought it looked a bit like Barbarella. I initially learnt sewing in school, but then I dropped out as the course was angled in an extremely uninteresting way.

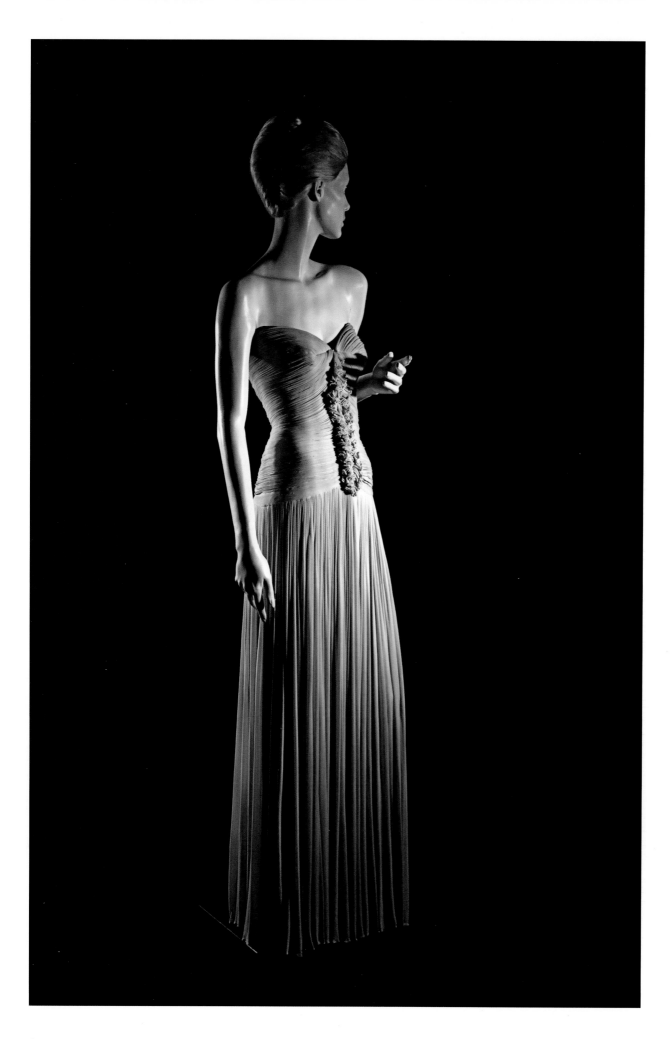

ON NANNIES

In England, the nannies in the park were dressed in uniforms. But times had begun to change. The old-fashioned nannies wore little hats, rather like Mary Poppins, but the young nannies, in their twenties, wore the new fashions. That was their uniform. When I was really little, I had a Japanese nanny. My mother says I could speak Japanese then, but maybe she exaggerated. However, my fascination with everything Japanese started there.

ON BIBA

My mother knew Barbara [Hulanicki] and when I was about five we lived right next door to [her boutique] Biba. My nanny used to take me to Biba to see the flamingos on the roof. It was great! Biba was always packed with teenagers, and there were all these cool people milling around, and incense was everywhere. I would come home from school and beg to go there.

ON PLAYING DRESS UP

When I was a child, playing dress-up was so much fun. You could be a knight one day and an Indian the next.

MIKAEL JANSSON

Daphne wearing Givenchy by
Riccardo Tisci jacket, top, and shoes
with her own pants (purchased at a
Dublin punk shop) and jewelry, 2009.
Photo © Mikael Jansson.

My mother's mother [Joan Lisney] was very good friends with Madame Grès, and Vionnet and Balenciaga. At one point, I was told that I might be going to Madame Grès's studio as an intern. That would have been so interesting. But she was already terribly old and it never came to anything. Also I was heading to Guildhall to become a singer. But then I looked at Madame Grès's clothes and photographs of her work, and I went to the British Museum to look at classical statues with drapery. If someone gives me an idea, I run with it. My imagination is vivid. Now, when I think of these things it fills me with regret, as I would have been fascinated to have had the practical tools to sew and embroider myself. Of course, I was a musician then first and foremost, but fashion dovetails into the world of art, music, and literature.

ON HER FIRST COUTURE SHOW AND DRESS

I went to one of Hubert [de Givenchy]'s shows with my grandmother. I think that was the first couture show I went to. The first couture dress I ever bought was probably the pony skin Lacroix with a bubble skirt in 1987, which I still have. I saw a picture of it in a magazine and I wanted to find out who Christian Lacroix was. Of course, you could say that Azzedine's clothes are like couture, and I wore those when I was a teenager.

Madame Grès,
evening dress, 1955, France
Gift of Mrs. E. L. Cournand,
The Museum at FIT 77.187.1
Photo copyright The Museum at FIT.

HER FATHER ON DAPHNE

Fast-forward to the present. Daphne has become an international fashion icon. I asked her father, Jonathan Guinness, Lord Moyne, what he makes of this development.

"A fashion icon? Yes, that seems quite clear. I have tracked her progress with interest, though not really with surprise. She was always artistic, able to transmit shapes to paper. She was always original, liable to come up with an unexpected comment. Her school said she was violent in playing lacrosse, which amused me, because she always looked exceptionally sweet and gentle. Mainly, as a schoolgirl, she was good at getting around regulations; she had a replica of the garden key made and used it to go out into the town. An individualist, then, but never a show-off.

"Her iconic status comes simply from doing her own thing and, because that thing seems unusual to some people, getting noticed. Another thing: I went with her once into a Paris fashion house and noticed that she was very friendly with the ladies who actually did the work; they all knew her, which to me indicates that she doesn't just use the finished product of fashion as an aid to self-assertion but is interested in the process of creation; fashion as a cooperative venture."

Daphne and father, Jonathan Guinness, on her wedding day in 1987. Photo courtesy Daphne Guinness.

My wedding dress was by Marc Bohan of Dior, but really I designed it. The dress had white fox trimming; I dreamt of Brittany lace and a bustle like a dress in a Tissot painting. Literally five minutes before the ceremony, I realized that I didn't have any shoes, so I had to run out and get some. You have to get married twice in France. For the civil ceremony, I wore a Chanel suit. Mr. Paquito was the Head Cutter at Chanel then. I learnt so much from all the incredible people in the ateliers. My favorite thing is to watch the process. This fascination could be applied to many of my pursuits.

Daphne was married from 1987 to 1999. She is reticent about these years, but there is the impression that it was something of a caged-bird period for her. Or, to use another metaphor, she was a pupa in a chrysalis, no longer the busy little caterpillar eating up inspirations, but not yet the fantastic butterfly that she would later become. Yet although she had a very private life in those years and dressed more conservatively than she would later, she was clearly still very interested in fashion.

[Left and Center]
Daphne Guinness on her wedding day.
Daphne's dress by Marc Bohan of Christian
Dior. Photo courtesy Daphne Guinness.

[Right]
Daphne Guinness at her civil wedding
ceremony wearing a blue Chanel suit.
Photo courtesy Daphne Guinness.

ON HER YEARS IN A WIFELY CHRYSALIS

When I was in school, when out of uniform, I wore pretty much anything I wanted. Then I got married – and it was fifteen years of having children and being quite conservative, which was interesting in itself. My husband was quite conservative, which I respected. He didn't like me to dress up. I'd buy Manolos and hide them. I'd take off my stilettos and put on flats. He didn't like me to wear hats – an English peculiarity which is almost inexplicable.

When I was married, I'd try to tone it down and dress in a way that my husband was comfortable with. Of course, having children played its part, and living in Switzerland was not conducive to dressing up. I would always be reading and drawing or singing out of sight, and I would wander in the mountains of the Engadine and dream of my ideas. I would walk to high peaks and listen to classical music and dream and have thoughts. We didn't really go out that much; we lived with his father all the time. That was fine, because my husband was fascinating and I adored him. I have so many interests, such as reading and politics, that it was just changing channels. I am never bored on my own.

When I channeled my creativity, I directed it towards men's clothes, which I love. I have an absolute passion for men's clothes, and I would go to Huntsman and other tailors, where I could rifle through their archives. I love white tie. I think white tie is so much more elegant and beautiful than black tie. Not to mention top hats! But it has to be the right top hat – I love brushing a silk top hat – and really narrow trousers.

I'd go to Charvet and make all manner of shirts. You have no idea how many different whites and grades of weave and weights of cotton exist! To me, it's all about the fit. I'd start with the shoulder and go down from there. The fit is so important. You have to be able to move around, but it also needs to be fitted correctly to look sharp.

RENÉ HABERMACHER

Daphne's jacket by Chanel;
top hat and shirt, Daphne's own.
Photos René Habermacher.

ON BLACK SKI BOOTS

Sportswear is great for doing sports, but not for anything else. In Switzerland I was hiking, skiing, snowboarding, and *langlaufing* – and if you're doing sports, of course you need certain functional things, preferably in black. But I had to look everywhere to find black ski boots. At that time cross-country ski boots were yellow, not my favorite color! Those yellow ski boots made me feel like a canary! I hated to look at my feet, and that combination of purple and turquoise that they use for ski clothes was hideous. I just wanted black.

I had to go back to my maiden name, and I had to construct something new. It was not a conscious decision [to change] – I reverted to type! Being oneself means being on one's own, and I was completely on my own. It was pretty frightening. I started off trying to disguise myself, but I discovered that the disguise was making me more visible.

When my children went away on holidays, I had a gap of three months yawning ahead of me. I didn't want to just hang out on the beach or garden, so I took different courses. I took life drawing at the Slade; I did Shakespeare at RADA, and Shakespeare again at LAMDA. I have always been obsessed by *Hamlet*. I did a politics course at University College London. I had a math tutor for a year. I read. I spend most of my time reading. Contrary to some people's perception, I am not a terribly social animal.

In retrospect, the years during which Daphne was married seem to have been something of a hiatus; a period during which, as she told me, "Ideas were flowing, but there was little to be done creatively." After her divorce, Daphne resumed her maiden name, and started working on some of her ideas. In a sense, she began to reinvent herself.

HAMISH BOWLES ON DAPHNE

Hamish Bowles, a British editor at *Vogue* US, provides insight into Daphne's evolution and her place in fashion history.

"Daphne Guinness represents a continuum with the rich tradition of British and Anglo-Irish women possessed of unique and idiosyncratic flair for fashion and dramatic self-presentation. In fact, she is related to a great many of them, from the multi-faceted Mitford sisters, to the madcap triumvirate of Jazz-Age Guinness sisters, Maureen, Oona, and Aileen.

"Throughout her marriage to the scion of a publicity-phobic dynasty, Daphne maintained an ardent engagement with the worlds of fashion and style, but, sequestered from the public eye as she was, her unique taste and flair remained unrevealed to all but her intimate circle.

"Her marriage over, Daphne moved from shadow to sunlight – or rather the Klieg-light glare of the paparazzi lens, and the camera sights of some of the most fashion-forward photographers of our age. Daphne's passion for fashion blossomed as the wider world discovered her whimsical flair, and her eye for

FRANÇOIS NARS

NARS Bento Box Campaign featuring
Daphne, Fall/Winter 2010–11
Photo courtesy François Nars/
The Collective Shift/trunkarchive.com

the unique. Daphne's instinctive sense of style is married to a probing intelligence – she finds poetry in clothes.

"She is in the tradition of the great fashion proselytizers – on the one hand nurturing young and sometimes even unknown creative talents, on the other setting a standard for established designers to live up to. She has the courage of her convictions and a rebel spirit of daring, as well as a flair for drama. As her butterfly wings have unfurled before us, Daphne has transformed herself into a constant fashion happening – and her own self-presentation into a unique form of fashion performance art. She is a continual inspiration."

DAPHNE ON ISABELLA BLOW

Isabella Blow was an influential fashion editor and flamboyant style icon. She is best known for discovering Alexander McQueen, whose entire graduate collection from Central Saint Martins she purchased for £5,000. She also had a close relationship with milliner Philip Treacy, and was known for wearing his hats. Issie was a good friend of Daphne, too, and when she committed suicide in 2007, it was deeply painful for Daphne.

I met Isabella Blow for the first time in about 1983 when I was sixteen. She looked nothing like she would later. Her grandmother was my great grandfather's mistress. I met her again in 1997 at my cousin's ninetieth birthday party. I was to go as a funeral pony, so Phillip Treacy and I concocted a hat with feathers coming forward. When she saw it, Isabella made a beeline for me. It is like magnetic forces at work when you meet someone who speaks the same language. She did amazing things as fashion editor at *The Sunday Times* and *Tatler*. She was very exacting and would get very frustrated with art directors, but I tried to keep out of that. I would be there with her, to be a brother-in-arms.

You never really worked with Issie – you were just suddenly in the middle of something. And then she'd disappear – and you'd be left holding the baby. The photographer would say "Where is Issie?" and I'd call and she'd say, "I'm having tea with a prince. I can't come. You do it!" So I'd do it. I didn't want to be on the payroll or on the masthead. She just had more fun when she had a friend with her. She really just needed someone who understood her references. Work and life were the same thing for Issie, and she was so enthusiastic!

DAVE BENETT

Isabella Blow and Daphne at the *When Philip Met Isabella* exhibition, July 2002. Daphen's top and pants by Marni; belt from flea market. Photo Dave M. Benett/Getty Images.

Issie always used to say, "You must meet Alexander McQueen – you'll love him." And I was always quiet, because I like to appreciate people by the things they do. I'm happy admiring their work; I don't need to be their best friend, you know. Then one day we ran into each other in Leicester Square. I was wearing his coat – the one with the dragon on the back that he made at Givenchy – and he came up to me and said, "That's the coat I made. My God! You bought that! Issie was telling me I had to meet you." After that we saw each other a great deal.

It was a friendship made in heaven, because we got along very well very quickly. I think he was under an enormous amount of pressure, and so busy, but we all managed to get together – Alexander, Shaun [Leane], Philip [Treacy], Issie, and David [LaChapelle]. The nicest thing was just having a cup of tea or a simple supper. That is when you can really share ideas, never at those big events.

I wish I'd mortgaged my house and bought everything that Alexander did at Givenchy. It was divine. I bought several things: the embroidered coat, a sequined dress . . . and many things from his own collection.

Alexander Lee McQueen was probably the greatest fashion designer of the contemporary era. He will be remembered both as a master tailor and as the creator of powerful and original fashions that evoked a kind of "savage beauty." Isabella Blow once said that McQueen was "like a Peeping Tom in the way he slits and stabs at the fabric to explore all the erogenous zones of the body." Always a rebel (he said that designers were not "lap dogs to the ladies who lunch"), McQueen had a tempestuous time at Givenchy and eventually left to concentrate on his eponymous collection. One of Daphne's closest friends, McQueen committed suicide in 2010, a week after the death of his beloved mother.

DAVE BENETT

Daphne and Alexander McQueen attend the after-party following the GQ Men of the Year Awards, September 2004. Photo Dave M. Benett/Getty Images.

We rarely talked about clothes, more about our personal lives, whatever crisis we were going through. He was terribly funny and very protective, and he cheered me up when I was sad. He'd come to my house and we'd go through my things. He loved looking at things and seeing how they were made. It was so fun. I did spend time with him in the studio and sometimes an idea or two would fly around. Once I said I wanted to see his take on the simplest dress possible, one that I could wear forever – and he did a mock-up in about five seconds.

I didn't go to every single fashion show. I loved the one with the wind tunnel. The Chessboard collection was incredible, and I loved Voss, the one with the glass cube. Alexander was unlike other designers in that he always wanted his friends and family at his shows. It wasn't just for editors and grand people. There was quite a theatrical, marvelous gang there.

To me, Alexander was always first and foremost an artist. There are people who make clothes and people who are artists; designers who are very good at ideas and designers who have the technical ability. But Alexander could do everything. He'd put in the hours to learn tailoring, but he was an artist. When you have a real foundation in something, it's a great advantage. You can't just be an airy-fairy artist; a great deal of structure is needed even for the simplest idea. It's all very well having lots of ideas, but if you can't execute them, it's very frustrating.

Alexander had very good people with him, but he could do everything himself. In order to break the rules, you have to know them first. Alexander could really cut and he had a real vision. And he understood the human body. I tell my children that the really great inventions come when people have crossed disciplines; if you have an understanding of, say, mathematics or physics and then you also have an artistic side, for example. That's when you can do something truly original – whether in art or fashion or whatever, that's when you can make a great leap forward, rather than just continuing to reference the past. It is one of the saddest losses to my life that Alexander died.

MIKE MARSLAND

[Left] Daphne attends the memorial service for Alexander McQueen, September 2010. Daphne's dress by Alexander McQueen and hat by Philip Treacy styled with Daphne's jewelry.
Photo Mike Marsland/WireImage

DAVE BENETT

[Right] Daphne attends the private view of *Anthony Gormley: Test Sites*, June 2010. Dress by Alexander McQueen. Photo Dave M. Benett/Getty Images

Couture is the historical link through which knowledge about fashion is passed down from person to person. Without support, it is in danger of disappearing, like a forest of oaks that could never be replaced if it were cut down. A lot of people think I wear only couture, but unless you're a Saudi princess you can't afford to wear it all the time. Thank God I'm a sample size!

Daphne believes that couture is an art form that should be supported. As a client, she is also very conscious of the many skilled craftspeople whose work contributes to the final dress. She has said that "The thing about haute couture, unlike prêt-à-porter clothing, is that you actually have to engage with the process and repeatedly go for fittings." The process also allows her to contribute her own ideas, and she loves nothing more than creative collaboration. But she is also willing to wear a designer's most outrageous creations, unlike most couture clients who prefer to tone things down.

DOMINIQUE MAÎTRE

Daphne at the Chanel Haute Couture show for Fall/Winter 2008/2009 collection in the Grand Palais, Paris, July 1, 2008. Daphne's dress by Chanel. Photo Dominique Maître.

ON KARL LAGERFELD

Karl Lagerfeld is the most successful couturier working today, and the man who has made Chanel the world's leading luxury brand. Daphne has purchased many couture garments from Chanel, and she wears her favorite clothes repeatedly. She says, for example, that she has worn one Chanel coat-dress about fifty times.

The great thing about Karl is: he gets it. I'm not a Chanel handbag person, but I'm into Karl's aesthetic. We both wear these very high collars, lots of rings, and shrunken suits, and the white hair. I admire the thoroughness of Karl's cut, the perfection of his shows, and the devotion of his team, with whom I have built a strong relationship. It was so clever of Chanel to buy Lesage, because who else knows how to embroider with that level of skill?

MARIO TESTINO

Daphne wearing Chanel Haute Couture.
Photo Mario Testino/Art Partner
for *Vogue* UK, March 2008.

VALENTINO ON DAPHNE

Valentino Garavani has dressed all of the world's most beautiful women — from Jacqueline Kennedy and Grace Kelly to Farah Diba . . . and Daphne Guinness. He won their support because his dedication to the techniques of the couture, together with his exquisite taste, has resulted in extraordinarily beautiful clothes. This consummately sophisticated figure is one of Daphne's great admirers. "Daphne amazes me all the time," Valentino told *W Magazine*. "When I think she has reached the best, she comes up with something better."

"Daphne is like a beautiful flower. When I first met her, she was a very sweet, shy young girl, who did not seem very interested in dresses and jewels. She was blond, natural blond, and very, very pretty. Over time she has become like an extravagant, sexy, luscious, marvelous flower . . . Life is a stage for Daphne. She can steal the show from every other girl in the room, but they don't mind, because she's so sweet that everybody has to love her."

Valentino is such a sweetheart. I love him so much. I've known him since when I was just married. Valentino has the aesthetic of timeless beauty that so few people still have. He likes his women to look beautiful. Valentino always tells me that he loves to see what I'm going to wear. It is very flattering. He says, "I can always tell where you've been because of the trails of feathers and beads." I really like and wear my stuff.

ERIC RYAN

Daphne attends the Chanel fashion
show during Paris Fashion Week
Haute Couture Spring/Summer 2009,
wearing a modified Chanel dress and
Azzedine Alaïa belt. Photo Eric Ryan/
Getty Images.

ON AZZEDINE ALAÏA

Azzedine was one of the first designers I met. What I love about his design is that it hasn't changed very much; his attention to detail is beyond a passion, and his things are so beautifully constructed. He's the master of fit, and I like to feel a perfect fit. He's an artist. He shows his latest collection when he's ready, not just because it's fashion week. Trends come and go, but if it's right, it's always going to be right. If you're really engaged with something – whether it's a book, a picture, or a piece of clothing – you're always going to like it.

Among the designers whom Daphne admires most are those, such as Azzedine Alaïa, who do not, officially, create couture, but whose work might be described as demi-couture.

ON JOHN GALLIANO

I have some of the early pieces that John did at Dior. He did a collection inspired by Poiret that was so great! Those opera coats and the accessories! And I loved the French Revolution collection; it's one of my favorite collections. He also did exquisite lingerie at Dior. Oh, God, I love lace! And embroidery. Actually, I love anything that has so much work and love put into it. That's why I like the espadrilles you get in Spain. They only cost about two euros, but they're finished by hand, and they are better than the French ones that are finished by machine. Obviously most things have to be made by machine, but you can add some sort of hand detail. You don't have to settle – even if you just change the buttons yourself.

Daphne's collection includes relatively few, but extremely important, looks by John Galliano for Christian Dior Haute Couture. Typically, Daphne focused on his most poetic and extreme creations.

ON CORSETS

I love putting on corsets, getting really squeezed in.

NICK HARVEY

[Left] Daphne attends the Maison Martin Margiela "20" Exhibition, June 2010. Dress by Daphne and hat by Philip Treacy. Photo Nick Harvey/WireImage.

DAVE BENETT

[Above] Daphne attends the Istancool arts festival by Liberatum Saturday lectures, July 2010. Dress by Daphne and hat by Philip Treacy. Photo Dave M. Benett/Getty Images.

"Daphne is a designer's dream. She is the ultimate fashion animal. Designers think in terms of the ultimate, and Daphne is above and beyond every other couture customer. She looks better than the runway model – exquisite, unbelievable. You never look at Daphne and think 'She's wearing X' – because she makes the clothes her own.

"She's as sharp as razor blades, highly intelligent, very cultured, and she knows everything about fashion – from collar to cuffs. She knows what is good – what good is – and she knows exactly what she wants. She wants something that has never been seen before – and that's a tall order. She made these Duchess of Windsor dresses with Alexander McQueen. He made them on her figure, which is beyond mannequin, and they worked together very closely.

"Daphne's passion for fashion is unquantifiable. It's a life-and-death situation for her – which sounds ridiculous, but for people who live for fashion, it's inspiring. It's also intimidating! I've never told her this, but making something for Daphne can be a bloody nightmare for me – even though she's one of the sweetest people in the world – because I don't want to disappoint her."

The milliner Philip Treacy is one of Daphne's closest friends and a long-time collaborator, who made her a hat with feathers inspired by a funeral pony. I telephoned him to speak about Daphne, and almost the first words out of his mouth were: "Issie had a heart and Daphne also has a heart."

DAPHNE ON PHILIP TREACY

He's always got a thimble on his finger – and he's always working. When I go to his atelier, we'll be working until four in the morning. He'll teach me how to steam a feather.

ON DESIGNING CLOTHES

In addition to collaborating with designers, Daphne also designs her own clothes. In fact, she says that she designs "constantly" – making hundreds of garments, including shirts, skin-tight trousers, feathered capes, and frock coats. She has also "been trying to make a pair of robot legs-style leggings for years" and she was very impressed by Balenciaga's gold metal-look trousers. Although she proudly says that she knows how to use a sewing machine, she typically has her clothes made by tailors and dressmakers.

A few years ago, Adrian Joffee of Comme des Garçons asked Daphne if she would like to design something for Dover Street Market, Rei Kawakubo's experimental clothing emporium in London. A great admirer of Kawakubo's avant-garde fashions, Daphne agreed, and in 2007 she created her own clothing line, called Daphne, in collaboration with Dover Street Market.

I had been making shirts with Charvet and Turnbull & Asser and Jeeves & Hawkes. You really have to go to a men's tailor to get a shirt done well. If you go to Charvet, it's a wall of white – so many weights and weaves, you get to see Sea Island cotton and linen. They probably all look the same to everyone else, but they are all just slightly different, and I like that. I always like shirts with very long sleeves and a high collar, and I like the inside as much as the outside.

One day I was having lunch with Adrian, and he said: "Why don't you make some of those shirts for me?" For Dover Street Market, I started making shirts with Anthony Price, but the problem with making them in London is the price point. Dover Street Market has taken over the production – thank God!

Frock coats and tails – that's the next thing I'm working on. The starting point is Victorian, but I'm making it sharper. Too many ruffles can overwhelm you. I took a Victorian coat recently, and moved the beading from the outside to the inside.

I didn't just decide one day, "I want black and white hair." It happened in stages. I began as a blonde. I combined the lightest blonde and the darkest brown. People started saying I look like Cruella de Vil, but I've never even seen *101 Dalmations*.

Daphne's stylized self-presentation goes far beyond her clothing. From her striped hair (often adorned with diamonds) to her killer shoes, she looks completely original.

ON HER SHOES

I've always wondered how to play with my height – five foot five-and-a-half inches. I just wanted to be able to look people in the eye. Also, trousers look more elegant with an extended leg. So I used to go to strip shops and buy platform shoes. Manolo [Blahnik] has given me hell about "those ugly shoes you wear," but I love my platforms. Of course, I love my Manolos, too. I've been going there for years and his shoes are sculpture.

Unfortunately, men don't like platform shoes. Since I've been wearing platforms without heels, now I can no longer walk in heels because I catch the heels in the pavement. If these were not comfortable, I would not be wearing them. But they are comfortable. I have some shoes that I wear every day and others that I look at, but I tend to get a lot of repeats, multiples of the same style.

Daphne is especially notorious for her sky-high shoes. She is one of very few people who can walk in McQueen's Armadillo shoes, for example. In recent years, she stopped wearing high heels and started wearing amazingly high platform shoes without heels. She gets many of them especially made in Paris by Christian Louboutin, and she has also started commissioning custom-made heel-less platforms from Japanese shoemaker Noritaka Tatehana.

DAVE BENETT

Daphne Guinness attends the semi-finalists announcement for The Dorchester Collection Fashion Prize, July 2010. Jacket by Daphne Guinness, dress by Daphne Guinness and Alexander McQueen. Photo Dave M. Benett/Getty Images.

ON AUCTIONING HER CLOTHES FOR CHARITY

In Spring of 2008, Daphne selected almost one thousand items of clothing and accessories from her personal archive to be auctioned off to benefit Womankind Worldwide, an international charity dedicated to helping women who have been the victims of political and domestic abuse. There were fashions, sometimes quite spectacular, by the likes of Alaïa, Chanel, Dolce & Gabbana, Gucci, Lanvin, McQueen, Valentino, and Versace, as well as shoes and boots by Jimmy Choo, Prada, and Yves Saint Laurent. "In the end, I went a little overboard," she told Eric Wilson. "I probably am getting rid of more than I envisioned originally. But the whole point is that you can't just give away your old rubbish. That's just not interesting at all."

Held at Kerry Taylor Auctions in London, the sale raised more than $150,000 for Womankind Worldwide. It also inspired Daphne to make her first experimental film, *The Phenomenology of the Body*, which explored the politics of clothing. Models were dressed as thirteen archetypal women – from Eve to Madame Mao – in the clothing of various historical eras. Some, such as Joan of Arc and Marie Antoinette, were obvious victims. More ambiguously, there was also an anonymous 1950s housewife. Each model was shown slowly revolving on a turntable.

DOMINIQUE MAÎTRE

Daphne with André Leon Talley at the Hotel de Crillon in Paris for the opening of *The Phenomenology of the Body*, pictures and movie exhibition, July 1, 2008. Daphne's dress by Alexander McQueen. Photo Dominique Maître.

Daphne has always created her own perfumes by mixing essential oils. One day at lunch, Adrian Joffe suggested that she create a fragrance in partnership with Comme des Garçons. The limited-edition fragrance, called Daphne, is a combination of bitter orange, incense, saffron, oud, jasmine, and tuberose. It took two years to create the scent, which was launched in 2009.

"Scent can take you on a journey, transporting you to places deep in your memory," said Daphne, who decided to make a film relating to it. "It is not an advertisement for the perfume," Daphne said. "It is a film inspired by the scent." The film, *Mnemosyne*, features ambiguous images of a woman's body, flowers, and coral, veiled in smoke. Co-directed by Daphne and David Parker, the film was nominated for a Webby Award (honoring excellence on the internet), in the experimental category.

In addition to directing *The Phenomenology of the Body* and *Mnemosyne*, Daphne also produced Sean Ellis's Oscar-nominated 2004 short, *Cashback*. Together with her friend, Joe Lally, she is currently working on two experimental films, *The Murder of Jean Seberg* and *The Black and White Maze of the Painted Zebra*. She also collaborated with Markus Klinko & Indrani on the video *Tribute to Alexander McQueen*.

MARKUS KLINKO & INDRANI

[Right] Daphne wearing cat suit by
Hogan McLaughlin. Photo Markus Klinko
& Indrani, styling and creative
direction by GK Reid.

[Facing] Daphne wearing Alexander
McQueen tights, shoes by Hogan
McLaughlin and her own cape.
Photo Markus Klinko & Indrani,
styling and creative direction
by GK Reid.

DAPHNE ON PHOTOGRAPHERS AND FILM-MAKERS

Daphne likes nothing better than collaborating with other creative people, and she has worked closely with photographers such as Steven Klein and David LaChapelle. Klein's photo-shoot for *Vogue* Italia, "Future Couture, Starring Daphne Guinness," was especially successful.

I never know what I'm doing until I'm on set. I just get possessed. I'm happy in the process of creating something, whether photographs or film. If the artist wants you to do something, I want to be as accommodating as possible. He has his vision, and I like to do my best. I'm a tough little thing! You can ask me to do anything on set, and I'll do it. But when Steven dyed my hair black . . . I wasn't very happy. Everyone said, "Why did you do that?!"

ON STEVEN KLEIN

Steven Klein also photographed Daphne when she became the face of Akris in 2009. Albert Kriemler, designer for the venerable Swiss fashion label, chose Daphne because he thought she was "a beautiful and intriguing woman – a fashion icon in her own right." He had seen her photographed before by Steven Klein, and thought she emanated "a sense of mystery and aristocracy."

Another famous shoot was the David La-Chapelle advertising campaign for Maybach, the luxury German car manufacturer.

Steven [Klein] says he saw me at a show in Paris and thought, "Who's that interesting-looking girl?" He was a great friend of Alexander's. I did a picture with him in LA, of me sprawled by a pool with two dogs. He said: "Just bring some evening clothes." So we did that one.

Steven and Joe Lally came up with the idea for the *Vogue* Italia feature, "Future Couture." It was based on *The Birds Come To Die in Peru*, a lost film for Jean Seberg. Romain Gary, a French writer who was Jean Seberg's husband, did it out of love for her. The film was made in 1966 or '67, and has been completely lost, although the script and some still photographs do exist. It was about a diplomat and his wife, who's a frigid nymphomaniac. Steven and Joe wanted to do a remake of this lost movie, how we imagined the film must have been, with me playing the Jean Seberg character. They said, "Would you be available to do this?"

The couture was from that season, but I used a lot of my own things to accessorize. Patti Wilson styled it, but I always take a suitcase of my own stuff, because I don't feel comfortable in a lot of things. Philip [Treacy] made the headdress. The tide was coming in, and they said, "You're going to get wet," and I just threw myself in the water and it looked great. One model passed out because of the heat, and I was wearing a flipping cashmere dress!

Some people just want to hang around fashion, but it's very, very, very hard work! Some people don't do anything; they just stand around gawking. But there are also the most marvelous people. Patti's assistant would *carry* me across the beach, because I couldn't walk in the sand in high heels. These are the unsung heroes, so dedicated. It takes an enormous amount of work from everybody, and when something goes wrong, it is usually because someone is not doing their job right.

STEVEN KLEIN ON DAPHNE

"Dahpne Guinness – like navigating a tornado."

From "Future Couture, Starring
Daphne Guinness." Featured in
Vogue Italia, September 2008.
Daphne is wearing Dior haute
couture, eye patch by D'Argento
and shoes by Alexander McQueen.
Photo Steven Klein courtesy
Steven Klein and *Vogue* Italia,
September 2008.

From "Future Couture, Starring
Daphne Guinness." Featured in
Vogue Italia, September 2008
Daphne is wearing Valentino
couture dress and headpiece
with plume by Philip Treacy
Photo Steven Klein courtesy
Steven Klein and *Vogue* Italia,
September 2008.

From "Future Couture, Starring Daphne Guinness." Featured in *Vogue* Italia, September 2008. Daphne is wearing Giorgio Armani. Photo Steven Klein courtesy Steven Klein and *Vogue* Italia, September 2008.

From "Future Couture, Starring Daphne Guinness." Featured in *Vogue* Italia, September 2008. Daphne is wearing Chanel Haute Couture. Photo Steven Klein courtesy Steven Klein and *Vogue* Italia, September 2008.

DAPHNE ON DAVID LACHAPELLE

David always calls up and says, "Daffles, will you just pack a suitcase and we'll do a little project?" Once we were in a wax museum for three days and I had to wear white contact lenses – and my eyes bled. I just love working with him! He's absolutely fascinating to work with, because he knows it all – the Old Masters, the hair, the make-up, everything.

DAVID LACHAPELLE

"Daphne Guinness in Water,"
Los Angeles, CA 2008.
Daphne's dress by Lanvin.
Photo David LaChapelle.

"Exposure of Luxury," Maybach Ad Campaign, 2009.
Daphne's dress by Alexander McQueen.
Photo David LaChapelle.

"Berlin Story," Maybach Ad Campaign, 2009.
Daphne's dress by Alexander McQueen.
Photo David LaChapelle.

I have always loved armor. I think it's very beautiful to be able to cover yourself in metal. I love the color of it and the way it reflects light. But it is also a protection. You don't want to go around in some awful sort of yellow fire vest. You want to look chic.

When I started making the metal gauntlet with Shaun [Leane], I told him I wanted to look like I had been in a very chic road wreck. It has been such a long time since anyone's made a piece of armor. The gauntlet is not jewelry; it is sculpture. It is made of gold, platinum-plated diamonds, and chain mail.

Daphne is known for her "obsession" with armor, which began in childhood when she used to play among suits of armor at home. She often wears heavy metal jewelry, including metal gauntlet gloves that she designed herself, and she has collaborated with the jeweler Shaun Leane on a very special diamond-studded couture armor gauntlet glove. Tom Ford laughingly told *Vogue* UK, "I wouldn't be surprised if, one day, Daphne was buried in a diamond suit of armor."

RANKIN

[Facing] Daphne Guinness; glove by Shaun Leane for Daphne Guinness. Photo Rankin/ trunkarchive.com.

TIM BRIGHTMORE

[Right] *Contra Mundum*, a one-of-a-kind 18ct white gold and diamond glove by Daphne Guinness and Shaun Leane, 2011. Photo Tim Brightmore.

Sometimes I'm having fun and I think everyone will get it, and I don't understand why people say I'm eccentric. Hang on! I'm not eccentric! I'm very level-headed. Not eccentric, *imaginative*! When people say you are eccentric, they are trying to do you down or say you're crazy.

"English eccentricity is not crazy," says Philip Treacy. "It's a very subtle, underground cool. Daphne's personality is quintessentially English. She's the most English person I know."

Daphne *hates* being described as "eccentric" – but the word appears in almost every article about her.

SUZY MENKES ON DAPHNE, COUTURE, AND MAD HATS

Suzy Menkes, Fashion Editor of the *International Herald Tribune*, provides an informed perspective on Daphne's significance in the world of fashion. She also compares her to Isabella Blow, noting the differing reactions of the Americans and the English to such individual figures.

"It must be heart-warming for couturiers and exceptional fashion designers that Daphne Guinness is prepared to wear their clothes as shown, as if she were part of a fashion show brought to life. For so long now, ever since high fashion and haute couture have been used as brand marketing tools, the lovers of couture, at least, have worked with the vendeuse to make the clothes wearable. So Daphne becomes a living conduit of fashion at its most purely creative.

"It is interesting to me that Daphne only really came onto the scene after Isabella Blow had disappeared. Daphne is very elegant, a society figure and super rich – and Isabella was none of these things. But to a general public, I think it's mostly about mad hats. In America, anyone who wore a fancy hat in public would be considered completely weird. Ditto the Daphne shoes. The fashion world does throw up these figures: I once saw front row at a London fashion show Isabella, Zandra Rhodes, and the Italian Anna Piaggi. Naturally, in England, nobody stared or took any notice of any of them!"

STEVEN MEISEL

Daphne Guinness; veil headpiece by Yestadt Millinery; earrings and finger stalls by Erickson Beaman. Orginally featured in *Vogue* Italia, February 2010. Photo © Steven Meisel/Art+Commerce, courtesy Steven Meisel and *Vogue* Italia, February 2010.

RABBANI AND SOLIMENE

[Above] *AnOther Magazine* party
September, 2008. Daphne's necklace
by Lanvin. Photo Sherly Rabbani
and Josephine Solimene/
Rabbanisolimene.com

DAFYDD JONES

[Left] Daphne Guinness at Nicky Haslam's
Birthday Party. Daphne's necklace by
Tom Binns; headpiece by Philip Treacy
and vintage dress. Photo Copyright
© Dafydd Jones, www.dafjones.com.

Some of it I inherited and some I bought; some is real and some is fake. I like to mix real and fake diamonds, and no one can ever tell the difference. Once I ironed a lot of crystals onto a jacket, and everyone just assumed they were real diamonds. The press said, "She's covered with diamonds."

I like vintage 1920s and 1930s Cartier or Van Cleef and Arpels, because they are set so well that they never break. You can swim in them, whereas with eighteenth- and nineteenth-century jewelry, the stones can fall out. I like black or red lacquer with gold, but lacquer is fragile. I like to wear lots of brooches. I also design quite a lot of jewelry.

I like going to thrift markets and finding old bits and pieces. You can find good fake diamonds in Chinatown if you look. If it's not too symmetrical and the metal is slightly blackened, it looks real.

I hate to keep things in the bank. When are you going to wear your jewelry if not now? When you are dead? Best is for every day!

ON SPORTSWEAR

The invention of sportswear is the worst thing that happened to fashion, and not just because it looks sloppy. It's because people took it as an excuse to wear it all day long, and that was not the point. The point is to wear it to get in shape, not to wear it after you've stopped working out. When men drink beer and wear sweatpants, it's the beginning of the end. The suit was a very good thing for men.

Daphne made headlines when she revealed that she wears a white t-shirt and black leggings by Rick Owens – to work out at the gym.

ON FIT

My rule of thumb is to get my clothes always a little too small. Most people wear their clothes far too big. It looks undignified. People should just take their shoulders in an inch or two. I cut my clothes from the bones on my shoulders. Your clothes should fit quite neatly to you, whether they are made for you, or you alter them yourself. Also I think about the whole silhouette being in one piece. You don't want to end up cutting yourself in the wrong place; then you look shorter. You can be four-foot eleven and look six foot if you get it right. You should try to keep everything very, very skinny.

RABBANI AND SOLIMENE

Daphne attends dinner party for Zac Posen for Mercedes-Benz Fashion Week Spring 2009, September 2008. Daphne's outfit by L'Wren Scott. Photo Sherly Rabbani and Josephine Solimene/WireImage.

ON INSPIRATION AND IMPOSTERS

I am often inspired by art. I see a Gainsborough at the Wallace Collection, and I think "God! I love that sleeve!" Or I go to Portobello Market and try to find something, such as a bit of lace. Just being a beagle.

In the past there seemed to be a code, and you could tell from people's appearance which tribe they came from, which movies and books they liked. But now there are so many imposters, and it is easy to think '"Why are you dressed like that?" It's good to take inspiration from something, but you should know why you are taking inspiration from it and not just mindlessly reference it for no apparent reason. Today people in the industry say "Look at this film so you can do a shoot based on it."

ON CROSS-DRESSING

It's nice to be different people. I'd like to be able to change gender. I want to be Oscar Wilde or Georges Sand. There is so much cross-dressing in Shakespeare. I'm inspired by that. I was probably one of the only women customers at Huntsman. They have all their patterns from the past 150 years. In my next life, I'll be a tailor.

RANKIN

[Above] Daphne's belt by Alaïa,
top hat and shirt Daphne's
own. Photo Rankin/
trunkarchive.com.

DAVE BENETT

[Right] Daphne attends the British
Fashion Awards, November 2006.
Daphne's dress by Chanel and
necklace by Christian Lacroix.
Photo Dave M. Benett/
Getty Images

I can't imagine that I'm a muse. "Muse" is like a title. I've never been asked to be a muse. The term "muse" is used for someone like Amanda [Harlech] with Karl. I'm not allied or identified enough with one designer – I'm more like a bee, going from flower to flower. I just want to have fun. If someone takes inspiration from me, that is very flattering. Humans do mimic each other.

MARY MCCARTNEY

Daphne wearing her own
vintage sequin jacket.
Photo Mary McCartney.

"Daphne is one of – if not the – most stylish women living. Her style is completely unique and often eccentric, but her keen understanding of her looks, her body, and most importantly her character and personality, make everything that she wears feel as though it has been made for her – and, of course, in many instances it has. Daphne has a reverence for clothes and for fashion, yet at the same time she realizes that other things in life are much more important and so she has no fear when it comes to dressing, and this fearlessness and total security with who she is as a woman creates a dazzling character. Daphne is a true fashion original. She is one of a kind."

Designers certainly continue to find inspiration in Daphne. After he left Gucci, Tom Ford took a break from designing fashion to focus on film-making. But when he returned with his own eponymous collection, Daphne was "over the moon about Tom's return." And when he asked her to model in his fashion show, she felt that she "couldn't refuse him, even though I'm the shyest person on earth." Dressing Daphne for his Spring/Summer 2011 collection, Ford acknowledged both her love of structure and her ability to "pull off" even the most dramatic looks.

TOM FORD

Daphne wearing Tom Ford dress.
Portrait by Tom Ford.

DAPHNE ON GARETH PUGH

Daphne has also developed a relationship with the edgy young designer Gareth Pugh, whose futuristic clothes, characterized by body-conscious lines and geometric cuts, are the most exciting styles to have come out of Britain in recent years. "Daphne is one of those people who really knows what she wants," Pugh told *Time Out* London. "She's an iconic, fashion-forward, thinking kind of person . . . She's a very big supporter of creativity." Backstage at one of Pugh's shows in Paris, Daphne told a Brazilian journalist: "Gareth is indisputably the best cutter and the most future-forward designer we have."

Gareth is incredible. He is obviously very different from Alexander, but [like McQueen] he has a vision of his own. He is not just referencing the past. He made an amazing dress for me out of sliced Lycra, and I had to change into it in the back seat of a taxi – not easy!

BRYAN ADAMS

Daphne Guinness; dress by Gareth Pugh; gloves by Charlie le Mindu; headpiece by Philip Treacy; shoes by Giorgio Armani. Originally featured in *Zoo Magazine*, issue 29, November 2010. Photo Bryan Adams/ trunkarchive.com.

I don't really have any style icons, just people I think who are extremely individual and fascinating to look at, such as the Duchess of Windsor, Jean Tierney, and Jean Seberg. And gender-bending rockers, like Jimi Hendrix and David Bowie. But I don't want to put anyone on an altar. I never thought I wanted to be another person.

When I was twelve or thirteen, we had an assignment to write about someone who, in our opinion, was an important historical figure. Everyone else wrote about people like Queen Victoria. I wrote about Nancy Cunard. The other girls said, "Who's Nancy Cunard?" My father thought it was the funniest thing. But I love Nancy Cunard!

MAN RAY

(1890-1976) © ARS, NY
Nancy Cunard. 1926. Gelatin silver print. 9.1 x 6.6 cm (3 9/16 x 2 5/8 in.). The Metropolitan Museum of Art, Ford Motor Company Collection, Gift of Ford Motor Company and John C. Waddell, 1987 (1987.100.131). Image copyright © The Metropolitan Museum of Art / Art Resource, NY ©2011 Man Ray Trust / Artists Right Society (ARS), NY / ADAGP, Paris

ON BUYING ISABELLA BLOW'S COLLECTION

In 2010, Daphne stopped the sale of Isabella Blow's wardrobe, just before it was auctioned off by Christie's, by purchasing the entirety of the lots. In an article for *The Financial Times* titled "Why I Stopped the Sale," Daphne explained her decision.

"The story begins on the morning of May 7, 2007, when I was woken in New York City at 4 a.m. by a telephone call from Alexander McQueen. I had been dreading but half-expecting this call for quite some time. Issie was dead, he said. She had poisoned herself.

"God knows, we – her sisters, her friends – had tried to stop this tragedy. I shall never get over Issie's absence, and when I heard that her estate needed to be settled so that her sisters could pay off her debts, the realization of what that would entail was really the last straw. The planned sale at Christie's could only result in carnage, as souvenir seekers plundered the incredible body of work Issie had created over her life. I know she would have hated it.

"Isabella was my friend when she was alive, and that fact is unchanged by her death, and as her friend I did not want anybody misappropriating her vision, her life, and her peculiar genius. I would like this unique collection, marked by her grace and the fact that it was so intimately hers, to allow people (whether students, lovers of fashion, historians) to remember her and benefit from her legacy."

I was so nervous – I thought I would faint! Then the zipper of the dress got stuck . . .

In spring 2011 Daphne embarked on an unexpected project: "to lift a piece of the curtain that came down when I stopped the sale of Isabella Blow's things last year." At the invitation of Dennis Freedman, the new creative director of Barneys, Daphne found herself agreeing to organize a display of part of Isabella's collection in the windows of Barneys, together with certain items from Daphne's own collection, in conjunction with the opening of the exhibition *Alexander McQueen: Savage Beauty* at the Costume Institute of the Metropolitan Museum of Art, New York. She also agreed to get dressed for the Costume Institute Gala in the windows – "me as performance art!"

ON BEING AN ARTIST

I wouldn't presume to call myself an artist. I don't think it's an accolade you can give yourself. It's for others to say. What is my art? I try to look neat and tidy.

"Daphne reminds me of [the Australian performance artist] Leigh Bowery. Her process is more like an artistic process than a fashion-directed process. She makes her work in an artistic way, not with a commercial dimension. A designer might wish for the kind of creative freedom she has. We live in such conservative, corporate times that just to look at her is invigorating."

A few months earlier, Guy Trebay of the *New York Times* had memorably characterized Daphne as "a kind of performance artist whose tool kit is her wardrobe." In reply, she told him, "I'm an artist, I suppose." When I spoke to them, however, they both stepped back a bit. But the famous art historian John Richardson, author of the magisterial biography of Pablo Picasso, had no hesitation in describing Daphne as an artist.

"What she does is art. I'm not an admirer of performance art as a rule, but hers is performance art of a rather special kind, rooted in dressmaking, rather than self-advertisement. She must be God's gift for a designer who needs a vehicle for extreme form. But you feel with Daphne that, if pushed, she could make all her own clothes. She has the knowledge. And it helps that Daphne is an exceedingly cultured woman. She has read everything – philosophy, history, and not just fashion history – and she has an extremely good eye, for art and photography as well as fashion. It is not merely that Daphne knows how to dress in a brilliant, original, and highly artistic way, but that she contributes to the whole culture of fashion. That is what I meant when I said that she is the object of her own creativity and her persona is her own masterpiece."

BRYAN ADAMS

Daphne wearing dress and cape by
Boudicca; ring by Chanel Haute Joaillerie;
wig, Daphne's own. Originally fearuded in
Zoo Magazine, issue 29, November 2010.
Photo Bryan Adams/trunkarchive.com.

DAPHNE ON BEIGE

Fashion today is becoming more *beige*. By that I mean that everyone and everything is starting to look the same – almost like a Mao uniform. We should be flying the flag for individuality.

There is nothing beige about Daphne, whose personal style is strikingly original in the way it combines haute couture elegance with an irreverence that evokes the great dandies and rock stars of the past. The sheer joy that fashion can provide is a motivating factor for Daphne, who once said: "I think you do have a more fun life if you wear beautiful clothes. There is a certain joy in it. Dressing well is an art and it shows respect to be neatly turned out."

DAVE BENETT

Daphne at The Serpentine Gallery
Summer Party, July 2006.
Daphne's jacket by Chanel
Photo Dave M. Benett/
Getty Images.

ON HER PERSONAL STYLE

I can never plan an outfit. I just don't know until I'm going out the door. I get it wrong about 60% of the time. But it's OK to make mistakes.

I don't do event dressing, because every day is an event.

I don't follow fashion, and I don't read fashion magazines.

I love anything that sparkles – I'm like a magpie!

My default look is a white shirt, a black jacket, black shiny leggings – and my shoes.

I like structure . . . with a bit of chaos.

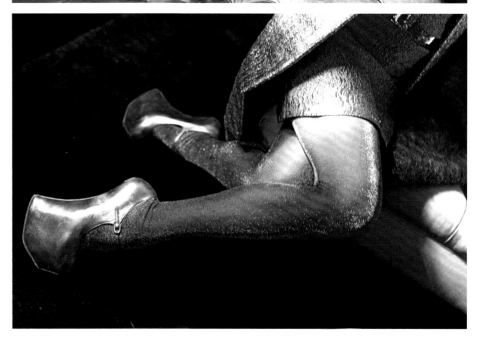

I think that fashion is one of the civilizing aspects of society. I treat clothes as art, although it is difficult to display them. At one point, I had acquired so many clothes that I thought: "I've got to get a handle on this." So I brought people in to catalog all the clothes, and put the photographs and information on a flash drive.

ALEX GEANA

Jacket and jewelry by Daphne
Photo Alex Geana for
Huffington Post

CONCLUSION

"People who collect clothes get a bad rap because they're told it's all vanity," says Daphne. Her own extraordinary collection of fashion encompasses many hundreds of important garments and accessories (quite apart from the Isabella Blow collection, which she saved from dispersal). "I collect clothes like people collect stamps or cars," she tells another journalist. Historically, it is quite true that collections of fashion have rarely been accorded the respect given to collections of art – or even cars or stamps.

Yet Daphne's collection is no mere assemblage of couture clothes, on a par with Imelda Marcos's thousands of shoes or the closets of a Saudi princess. It is not simply that her collection includes important couture looks by the greatest designers of our time, as well as cutting-edge garments by young designers. Her collection has a purpose beyond mere personal use. Although she obviously wears most of her clothes, she also buys fashions because she thinks they are beautiful and significant. She never intended to wear Isabella Blow's clothes, for example. Everything she acquires reflects her knowledge of, and respect for, the art of fashion.

Daphne's collection is a true repository of fashion creativity, and the fact that it is so well organized proved serendipitous when, in 2009, I asked her to collaborate with me on an exhibition that would present this collection and also convey the essence of her personal style. At first, she shyly declined. But then a few months later, as we walked through an exhibition at The Museum at FIT, Daphne asked me if I had been serious about her having an exhibition. I assured her that I would like nothing more, and after thinking it over, she agreed.

Daphne and I are co-curating the exhibition, with assistance from my colleagues Fred Dennis and Ken Nintzel. We chose approximately one hundred garments and accessories, including many by McQueen, as well as looks by Karl Lagerfeld for Chanel, John Galliano for Christian Dior, Valentino, Dolce & Gabbana, Azzedine Alaïa, and Gareth Pugh, among others. About half the clothes were stored in Daphne's London apartment and half in her New York apartment. In London, there was an entire large room filled with fashion, organized by designer and carefully hung on rolling racks with cloth dust covers. Both apartments were also amply supplied with closets, some devoted entirely to shoes or hats. There were also drawers of material, such as vintage lace.

The inspiration for the exhibition design came from the mirrored hallway in Daphne's New York apartment, and, more generally, from the symbolism of mirrors. The large gallery is divided by scrims and mirrors into a series of enclosed spaces flanking a central hallway, the totality evoking the idea of a hall of mirrors. With their hard, shiny metallic surfaces, they reflect Daphne's garments on display, as well as reflecting museum visitors looking at the garments. The scrims, which can be opaque or translucent depending on the light, evoke Daphne's use of veils as accessories, while also alluding to the concept of veiling as intrinsic to the mystery of clothing and fashion. The smaller entrance gallery features a small platform with one dress by McQueen, and a wall pierced with glass, behind which are displayed some of Daphne's accessories, including hats and shoes. Both rooms also feature projections and/or video screens depicting some of Daphne's films and videos, as well as a sequence of still images of Daphne. At the far end of the large gallery above the dresses, we have a life-size, moving hologram of Daphne.

DAPHNE ON HER EXHIBITION

What draws me to fashion is art . . . and certainly not fashion as status symbol. This exhibition is done for the benefit of those out there, students or otherwise, who share this love.

SELECTED BIBLIOGRAPHY

Armstrong, Lisa, "Daphne Guinness, Fashion's Invisible Muse," *The Sunday Times*, May 21, 2010

Blasberg, Derek, "The Real Daphne Guinness, *Harper's Bazaar*, March 2010

Cavendish, Lucy, "Daphne Guinness, Golden Girl," *Telegraph*, January 20, 2011

Davis, Maggie. "Gareth Pugh and Daphne Guinness," *Time Out* London, February 17, 2009

D'Souza, Christa, "Heiress Apparent," *The Sunday Times*, October 21, 2007

Fox, Chloe, "Couture Princess," *Vogue* UK, March 2008

Gill, A. A., "Study in Scarlet," *Vanity Fair*, March 2008

Grigoriadis, Vanessa, "Imagining Daphne," *New York Magazine*, August 15, 2010

Guinness, Daphne, "Why I Stopped the Sale," *The Financial Times*, July 3, 2010

Long, Carola, "My Life in Fashion: Daphne Guinness and Her Obsession with Armour," *The Sunday Times*, August 22, 2007

Reginato, James, "Rare Bird," *W Magazine*, March 2009

Schenzka, Joanne, "Daphne Guinness," *AnOther Magazine*, Autumn/Winter 2009

Wasem, Frances, "A Life in Style: Daphne Guinness," British *Harper's Bazaar*, October 2009

Williams, Sally, "Clothes auctions: Pret à vendre," Telegraph.co.uk, March 16, 2008

Wilson, Eric, "Daphne Strips Down," *New York Times*, April 24, 2008

Daphne Guinness – Style Icon at http://daphneguinness.tumblr.com/

www.markusklinko-indrani.com

www.vogue.it

www.vogue.com

Many people have helped to make this book possible, including Teresa Afonso, Primrose Dixon, Isobel Gorst, Jenna Kingma, Kate Ledlie, Steven Pranica of Creative Exchange Agency, and Laura Symons at Premier PR.

Our gratitude to the exhibition sponsors LEVIEV Extraordinary Diamonds, MAC Cosmetics, Jean Shafiroff, BNY Mellon Wealth Management, and The Couture Council, and also to our symposium sponsor, Barneys New York.

Sincere thanks to Hamish Bowles, Tom Ford, Jonathan Guinness, Suzy Menkes, John Richardson, Philip Treacy, Guy Trebay, and Valentino for their thoughtful remarks.

Thanks also to the photographers who have generously participated in this project: Bryan Adams, Dave M. Benett, Lorenzo Bringheli, Alan Davidson, Kevin Davies, Tom Ford, Alex Geana, René Habermacher, Nick Harvey, Nick Haymes, Mikael Jansson, Dafydd Jones, Steven Klein, Markus Klinko & Indrani, David LaChapelle, Joe Lally, Dominique Maître, Mike Marsland, Mary McCartney, Steven Meisel, Paul Morigi, Françoise Nars, Sherly Rabbani and Josephine Solimene, Rankin, Eric Ryan and Mario Testino.

And to all the assistants and agents who worked with us on this book: Samantha Beckett at Mary McCartney Studio, Bill Coate at Photographic Management Ltd., Lonyea Ellis at Getty Images, Mariella Ferrari at Valentino, Ziggi Golding at Z Photographic Ltd., Alessandra Greco at Philip Treacy, Steven Prancia at Creative Exchange Agency, Marc Rahr at Todd Shemarya Artists, Melissa Regan at Art + Commerce; Chelsea Rhadigan at Artists Rights Society, Tina Robinson at Trunk Archive, Adam Sherman at Steven Klein Studio, Julia Sloan at NARS Cosmetics Inc., Gregory Spencer at Art Partner, Jeff Stalnacker at Wilson Wenzel, Gayle Taliaferro at Trunk Archive, and Maria Walsh at Wilson Wenzel.

Many thanks to *Vogue* Italia, especially Franca Sozzani, Grazia D' Annunzio, Alice Furnari and Cristina Palumbo.

Thanks to everyone at the Museum at FIT who contributed their time and efforts to this project, especially Fred Dennis, Acting Senior Curator and Melissa Marra, Associate Curator of Education. Thanks also to Deputy Director Patricia Mears, the members of The Conservation Department, Ann Coppinger, Maria Fusco, Marjorie Jonas, The Exhibitions Department, especially Michael Goitia and Ken Nintzel, The Registrar's Department, especially Sonia Dingilian and Jill Hemingway, and The Curatorial Department, especially Editor Julian Clark, Museum Media Manager Tamsen Schwartzman, and Installer Thomas Synnamon. Thank you to the Curator of Education and Public Programs Tanya Melendez, Museum Photographer Eileen Costa, and Director's Office staff, Vanessa Vasquez, Varounny Chanthasiri, and Gladys Rathod. Thank you also to the interns who participated in this project: Marie Døllner, Laurie Filgiano, Emma Kadar-Penner, Krissia Sevilla, Paola Di Trocchio, and Rebecca Young.

Our gratitude to the Educational Foundation for the Fashion Industries, especially Dawn Duncan, Terry Culver, Kevin Hervas, Vicki Granowski, and Lindsay Yodice. Thanks to our graphic designer, Jen Pressley.

As always it has been a pleasure to work with Gillian Malpass and her colleagues Paul Sloman, Katharine Ridler, and Emily Angus at Yale University Press.

Valerie Steele & Daphne Guinness